DILEMMAS IN DEMOCRACY

Military Force

Derek Miller

Cavendish Square
New York

Published in 2020 by Cavendish Square Publishing, LLC
243 5th Avenue, Suite 136, New York, NY 10016

First Edition

Website: cavendishsq.com

Library of Congress Cataloging-in-Publication Data

Names: Miller, Derek L., author.
Title: Military force / Derek Miller.
Description: First edition. | New York : Cavendish Square, [2019] |
Series: Dilemmas in democracy | "A book for high school students about the use of military force and what it means for democracy both in the United States and around the world."--Provided by publisher. | Includes bibliographical references and index.
Identifiers: LCCN 2019000508 (print) | LCCN 2019002023 (ebook) |
ISBN 9781502645050 (ebook) | ISBN 9781502645043 (library bound) |
ISBN 9781502645036 (pbk.)
Subjects: LCSH: United States--Military policy. | War--Moral and ethical aspects. |
Militarism--United States. | Peace movements--United States. |
Civil-military relations--United States. | United States--Foreign relations--1945---
Citizen participation. | United States--Military policy--Citizen participation.
Classification: LCC UA23 (ebook) | LCC UA23 .M5636 2019 (print) | DDC 355.02--dc23
LC record available at https://lccn.loc.gov/2019000508

Editorial Director: David McNamara
Editor: Caitlyn Miller
Copy Editor: Alex Tessman
Associate Art Director: Alan Sliwinski
Designer: Christina Shults
Production Coordinator: Karol Szymczuk
Photo Research: J8 Media

The photographs in this book are used by permission and through the courtesy of:
Cover 501 Collection/Alamy Stock Photo; background (and used throughout the book) Artist Elizaveta/Shutterstock.com; p. 4 Marco Di Lauro/Getty Images; p. 6 Rainer Lesniewski/Shutterstock.com; p. 10 Rokas Tenys/Shutterstock.com; p. 11 Gal Istvan/iStockphoto.com; p. 13 Pierre Perrin/Gamma-Rapho/Getty Images; p. 17 Najim Rahim/AP Images; p. 20 Ahmad Al-Rubaye/AFP/Getty Images; p. 22 Isaac Brekken/Getty Images; p. 26 Erik Simonsen/Getty Images; p. 29 Peteri/Shutterstock.com; p. 32 Keystone/Getty Images; p. 34 PJF Military Collection/Alamy Stock Photo; p. 37 U.S. Forces when KSM was captured/Wikimedia Commons/File:Khalid Shaikh Mohammed after capture.jpg/Public Domain; p. 38 Staff/TNS/Newscom; p. 40 Wissam Al-Okaili/AFP/Getty Images; p. 42 Jefferson Siegel/Pool/Getty Images; p. 44 Joe Raedle/Getty Images; p. 46 John D. McHugh/AFP/Getty Images; p. 49 Popperfoto/Getty Images; p. 50 Rick Madonik/Toronto Star/Getty Images; p. 53 Joseph Eid/AFP/Getty Images; p. 54 Jonathan Jacobsen, Sophie Ramis/AFP/Newscom; p. 56 U.S. Navy/Getty Images; p. 58 Henry Warfield/Keystone/Getty Images; p. 63 Mark Wilson/Getty Images; p. 64 Harry Benson/Daily Express/Hulton Archive/Getty Images; p. 71 Irfan Khan/Los Angeles Times/Getty Images.

Printed in the United States of America

CONTENTS

CHAPTER 1

Using Military Force

The decision to use military force is one of the most important choices that a country can make. Wars cause immense human suffering. Soldiers leave home to fight on distant battlefields, and some do not return alive. No matter how careful soldiers are, innocent people die in every war. Men, women, and children cannot avoid the battles that rage around them or the bombs dropped on their cities. For these reasons, the question of whether to use military force is always a controversial one. In a democracy, the people must debate these issues and find the best way forward.

Debates About Military Force

The current "war on terror" is a perfect example of the debates that rage over the use of military force. On September 11, 2001, the United States suffered the deadliest terror attack on its soil in history. Terrorists hijacked four passenger planes to crash into targets on the ground. Two planes struck the

Opposite: An American soldier secures a building in Afghanistan before the country's 2009 elections.

The United States invaded Iraq and Afghanistan after the 9/11 terror attacks.

Twin Towers in New York City. The towers soon collapsed from the damage, killing many people trapped inside and rescuers trying to save them. Another plane struck the Pentagon—the headquarters of the military. The passengers on the fourth plane fought the hijackers after they heard about the attacks. Due to the passengers' heroic actions, the plane crashed into a field rather than its intended target. In all, nearly three thousand people lost their lives.

The 9/11 terror attack set in motion a series of events that continue to shape the world we live in. The American government quickly determined that known terrorist Osama bin Laden was responsible for the tragedy. He was living in Afghanistan, and the Taliban, a militant group that governed most of the country at the time, knew he was in the country. The United States led an invasion of Afghanistan to overthrow the Taliban and capture or kill bin Laden. This invasion was supported by most countries. It was seen as an act of self-defense after 9/11. American allies joined the effort. The Taliban was overthrown, and a new government was set up in Afghanistan. Controversially, some terrorists were captured and tortured for information.

In 2003, the American government, led by President George W. Bush, invaded a second country, Iraq, as part of the war on terror. Bush claimed that Iraqi leader Saddam Hussein had links to Osama bin Laden as well as illegal weapons of mass destruction (weapons like deadly gases and nuclear bombs). This time, the international community did not agree with Bush's claims. As a result, most other countries did not think the invasion of Iraq was justified.

For more than eight years, American soldiers would fight and die in Iraq. As more and more American soldiers lost their lives in the conflict, public opinion in the United States turned against the war. Civilian casualties—the deaths of innocent people caught in crossfire or accidentally bombed—became more widely discussed. Protests against the war also became more common, until troops finally withdrew in 2011. Meanwhile, American soldiers are stationed in Afghanistan to present day. Although they do not typically go on combat missions anymore, some still lose their lives each year in attacks.

The invasions of Iraq and Afghanistan highlight the dilemmas that democracies face when going to war. What is a good reason for going to war? Does a country need to listen to the international community when deciding to go to war? How many civilian casualties are acceptable? Do the benefits of war justify the sacrifices that men and women in uniform must make? Is torture ever acceptable?

These are questions the world and the United States are still trying to answer as the war on terror continues. Today, American combat troops operate in more than a dozen countries. In 2017, at least thirty-three American combat troops died overseas in countries stretching across Asia, the Middle East, and Africa.

In addition to combat troops, the United States uses airstrikes to target people and groups connected to terrorism. Bombs or missiles are dropped on distant targets in an airstrike. Between 2015 and 2018, American airstrikes were carried out in seven countries around the world. The president and military carry out airstrikes with little oversight. Some lawmakers and citizens argue there should be more debate about these methods of military force.

A Just War

The first question people ask before going to war is if it is the right thing to do. In other words, is there a good reason for starting a war or using military force in the first place? This is a surprisingly difficult question to answer in many cases. Often, citizens in a democracy will disagree on this point. Politicians may debate it as well. Both sides in a war usually believe they are in the right.

When it comes to deciding whether a war is just or legal, there are some international rules. Nearly all countries in the world belong to the United Nations (UN). The UN is an organization that helps countries work together and settle disagreements. One of the UN's main purposes is to secure world peace. In theory, the countries of the world have agreed to follow the UN's rules on war. In practice, these rules are often broken.

According to the UN, cross-border military force is forbidden in most cases. In other words, the military of one country should not enter another country. However, there are three exceptions to this rule:

- When one country asks another to send their military
- When military force is used in self-defense
- When the UN Security Council authorizes the use of military force (for example, in peace-keeping missions)

These rules seem simple, but applying them to the real world is difficult. A country may invite another country's military to their nation if the two are allies. Allies come to each other's aid when needed. Today, this is the reason that Russian soldiers are fighting in Syria. The dictator of Syria, Bashar al-Assad, invited Russia to fight armed groups who oppose his rule. Nonetheless, the United States and many other countries consider this use of Russian troops to be unjust. Critics argue Assad is not the legitimate leader of Syria because he is a brutal dictator. Therefore, they say his invitation is not a good reason for Russian military force.

Self-defense can also be very controversial. American president George W. Bush argued both the invasions of Afghanistan and Iraq were in self-defense. While the UN agreed with him in the case of Afghanistan, it disagreed on Iraq. These differences of opinion are frequent when it comes to self-defense. One country may believe war is necessary for its survival while other countries may think it is not.

NATO

NATO soldiers stand with the flags of some member countries.

Alliances play an important role in the use of military force. Countries agree to help each other when they are attacked. Ideally, this makes war less likely since weak countries have strong allies that will protect them. Throughout history, alliances have sometimes had the opposite effect. World War I began when a tangled web of alliances dragged all of Europe, and then the world, into war over a small dispute between two countries.

Today, the most important military alliance is the North Atlantic Treaty Organization (NATO). NATO is made up of twenty-nine countries including the United States, Canada, Turkey, and much

NATO members are shown here in blue.

of Europe. In the event a member is attacked, all twenty-nine countries promise to work together to fight the threat.

So far, this principle of collective defense has been used only once. After the 9/11 terror attack, NATO came to the defense of the United States. NATO participated in the war in Afghanistan. (NATO has also participated in other military operations even when no member is attacked.)

The militaries of NATO member countries practice working together. This makes NATO's command structure ready for military action when its members can agree on when to use military force.

In rare cases, countries may even get authorization go to war against an aggressor (a country that starts a war) that attacks someone else. This is what happened in the Gulf War. In 1990, Saddam Hussein invaded the neighboring country of Kuwait in an attempt to expand Iraq's borders by force. The United States responded by rallying international support to push Iraq out of Kuwait. After receiving authorization from the UN Security Council and a request from Kuwait, the American military acted. American troops drove Iraqi forces out of Kuwait.

The Gulf War was a military success. Some people even thought it would lead to a rule-based international order where unjust military force was always stopped by the international community. However, this has not been the case. The Gulf War remains one of the few wars in recent history that is not very controversial.

Authorization from the UN Security Council is the most straightforward justification for war. However, receiving authorization can be difficult. The council has five permanent members: the United States, Russia, China, France, and the United Kingdom. These permanent members have the power to veto. If a single permanent member votes against a decision, it does not pass. Ten nonpermanent members are also on the Security Council. For a decision to pass, it requires a majority of the fifteen members as well as agreement among the five permanent members. This level of agreement on the international stage is quite rare.

To further complicate matters, rules about when a country may go to war are not strictly enforced. There is no set penalty for breaking them. The UN Security Council may sanction a country for breaking them, but usually one of the five permanent members vetoes such an attempt. Sanctions are penalties applied to a country or its leaders. They may include limits on trade, travel bans for

Iraqi dictator Saddam Hussein in 1983

leaders, and bans on selling weapons to the country. More often than UN-backed sanctions, individual countries may apply sanctions against other countries.

Humanitarian Interventions

Aside from responding to aggression, another reason for going to war is for a humanitarian cause. Humanitarian interventions aim to save lives. Usually, they are meant to protect the people of a country from its own government or military. The legal basis for humanitarian interventions is sometimes shaky. They do not always meet one of the three reasons for cross-border force that the UN recognizes. Nonetheless, the international community often looks the other way when a humanitarian intervention is undertaken to save many lives in a crisis.

Humanitarian interventions sometimes become very controversial. This was the case in the country of Libya in 2011. Libyan dictator Muammar Qaddafi began killing people in his country when they protested—and later took up arms—against his rule. Qaddafi soon lost control of a large part of Libya. He sent the army to take it back and crush the revolt. It was at this stage that the United States, led by President Barack Obama, moved to intervene. Obama gathered the support of other countries and secured a UN resolution authorizing military force to protect civilians.

The United States and a coalition of other countries set up a no-fly zone, preventing Qaddafi's planes from bombing civilians. The United States and its allies also bombed the Libyan military as it moved across the country. This bombing campaign became so intense that some other countries began to criticize the United States. They said the United States was using the humanitarian intervention for "regime change." In other words, they believed

Obama wanted to remove Qaddafi from power, not just protect civilians. This went beyond the scope of the UN resolution. In the end, a convoy of vehicles Qaddafi was riding in was bombed, and he was pulled from the wreckage and killed.

Libya fell into chaos, and the United States and its allies soon stopped the airstrikes. Since these events, countries that opposed the killing of Qaddafi have been hesitant to authorize the use of military force to protect civilians. Unfortunately, the backlash against the 2011 intervention in Libya is not unique. Humanitarian interventions often face criticism that their real aim is not to save lives but to allow countries to interfere. Additionally, the inability of the United States and its allies to bring law and order to Libya after the death of Qaddafi shows the problems of military force. While preventing civilian deaths is good, outcomes are difficult to predict. Even wars started with good intentions can have bad results.

A Question of National Interests

While international rules about war are important, they are not the only factor in countries' military decisions. In fact, when a country debates going to war, the rules of the UN are often not the major issue. The main question is if a war is in the national interest. Many people believe that a country has the right to go to war if it is vital to its national interests, regardless of international law. National interests are important issues, like a country's safety and the economy. The question of whether national interests or international laws are more important is much debated.

In 2003, when President George W. Bush was preparing to invade Iraq against the wishes of the UN, many American citizens protested. They argued the United States should set an example to the world by following international laws. President Bush argued the invasion of Iraq was vital to the national interests of the United States. Therefore, he believed the UN could be ignored.

Today, this view that national interests matter more than anything else is seen in the actions of President Donald Trump's administration. American ally Saudi Arabia has been involved in a war in the country of Yemen since 2015. Saudi Arabia is fighting rebels in Yemen that are backed by Iran, a Saudi rival. In the course of the war, both sides have likely committed war crimes, according to a UN report. Saudi Arabia bombed civilian targets like hospitals and refugee camps. While this was happening, the United States was supporting the Saudi bombing campaign by helping them refuel planes and selling them arms.

At the end of 2018, the situation boiled over in the US Senate. The Trump administration argued that ties with Saudi Arabia were vital to national security interests. As a result, they said supporting Saudi Arabia during the war was necessary. UN concerns that they were killing civilians did not outweigh national security, Trump officials claimed. The Senate disagreed and passed a bill disapproving of the Trump administration's actions. While the bill is unlikely to get the president's signature and become law, it shows the fierce debate over what is and is not in the national interests of a country.

Civilian Casualties

Regardless of whether a country is justified in going to war, there are rules that they must follow. Every country in the world has signed the Geneva Conventions. The Geneva Conventions spell out how countries should act during a conflict. Conventions include rules like giving medical aid to captured soldiers, not using chemical weapons, and trying to limit civilian casualties. In general, the Geneva Conventions are widely accepted and not a topic of debate.

A man stands in the wreckage of a hospital that was accidentally bombed by the United States in Kunduz, Afghanistan. More than forty civilians lost their lives.

One issue that is controversial is how far to go in trying to limit civilian casualties. During a conflict, some civilian deaths are almost certain, but countries are supposed to take steps to make sure there are not too many.

The Iraq War is an example of how difficult limiting civilian casualties can be in practice. In the first two months of the conflict, an estimated seven thousand Iraqi civilians were killed. Airstrikes were responsible for most of these deaths. The United States military tries to avoid civilian casualties, but casualties still occur. Targets of airstrikes may be next to civilians, or bombs may not hit exactly where they are aimed.

Since the 2003 invasion, Iraq Body Count estimates that between 182,522 and 204,885 civilians have died in the conflict in Iraq as of December 1, 2018. Most of these deaths were not due to the United States or its allies but rather the forces fighting them. After US intervention, Iraq descended into a bloody civil war that saw huge numbers of civilian casualties. Still, this incredibly high civilian death toll shows the effect that starting a war has on ordinary people.

Rules of Engagement

The frequency of civilian casualties can be changed by the rules of engagement. These are the rules that pilots and soldiers on the ground follow. The president and military leadership are responsible for setting these rules. The rules spell out exactly how force should be used. For example, the rules of engagement determine whether bombs should be dropped on a house containing armed men if it is known that women and children are there as well.

In the ongoing conflict in Afghanistan, the American rules of engagement have changed multiple times. They were tightened by President Barack Obama, and his changes saw civilian casualties decrease. However, some politicians felt the new rules were too strict. They argued it made fighting back difficult. When President Trump was sworn into office, he relaxed the rules of engagement. This led to a sharp rise in the number of civilian casualties.

The debate over the rules of engagement and how many civilian casualties are acceptable is fierce. On the one hand, there is a desire to support soldiers and allow them to respond to threats. On the other, civilians need to be protected. They did not choose to live in a war zone. Citizens in a democracy are part of this debate. Throughout American history, many citizens have turned against wars when they felt too many innocent people were dying.

Looking at Different Kinds of Military Force

Issues surrounding going to war and civilian casualties look different depending on the conflict. In the modern world, countries use many different means of military force. The term "military force" refers to more than just large-scale war. The ability to bomb faraway countries, launch raids across borders, and hack distant computers have changed how countries interact with one another.

Invasion and Occupation

In the past, invasion was the usual method of exercising military force. An army entered another country, and soldiers waged a military campaign, fighting battles against the enemy and leaving men behind to guard ground that was taken. Before the development of long-range weapons, there was no alternative to this approach.

The American-led invasion of Iraq followed this model. Huge numbers of soldiers and tanks, supported by airplanes, invaded Iraq. These forces defeated Saddam Hussein's army. Afterward, American troops occupied Iraq. This means American soldiers stayed in the country and tried to stop armed groups from fighting.

A column of American tanks in Iraq in 2004

While invasion and occupation are what people tend to think of when they hear the words "war" or "military force," there are other important kinds of military force.

Light-Footprint Warfare

Frequently, military force takes the form of light-footprint warfare. Light-footprint warfare does not use large numbers of combat troops to fight an enemy and secure territory. Instead, special forces, airstrikes, and intelligence-gathering techniques are used to find and kill enemies. The development of unmanned aerial vehicles (UAVs)—or drones—made light-footprint warfare even easier. Now UAVs carry out airstrikes with no risk of a pilot being shot down over enemy territory.

Light-footprint warfare has many benefits. Casualties are lower than deploying a large number of combat troops. It is also cheaper for the military and government. The downside is that

The Legality of Targeted Killings

During the war on terror, the American government has been confronted by a problem. Some areas of the globe are lawless and difficult to reach, places where no government exercises authority. For these reasons, known terrorists can gather and are difficult, if not impossible, to capture. In response to these challenges, a program of targeted killings began. When capture is judged impossible, bombs and missiles are used to kill important targets instead.

This program of targeted killings is highly controversial. Thousands of people have been killed. The American government admits hundreds have been civilians. Critics say that number may very well be in the thousands. Civilian casualties are hard to count since the airstrikes occur in remote areas. According to supporters, targeted killings make terrorist networks weaker by killing their leaders. Opponents say they stoke the flames of hatred against the United States by killing civilians.

A further controversy is the killing of American citizens abroad in targeted attacks. According to the Constitution, citizens are entitled to a trial before punishment—in this case, execution. President Obama successfully argued that this was not the case for Anwar al-Awlaki, an American-born terrorist targeted to be killed. Lawyers representing al-Awlaki asked for a court decision, but their case was dismissed. Al-Awlaki was killed in an airstrike in 2011.

The targeted killing of American citizens is still hotly debated. Critics say it is unconstitutional, and it is illegal for the American government to kill its own citizens with no trial or public evidence of wrongdoing. Proponents say these targeting killings are necessary to keep Americans safe from terrorists.

AF
11 126

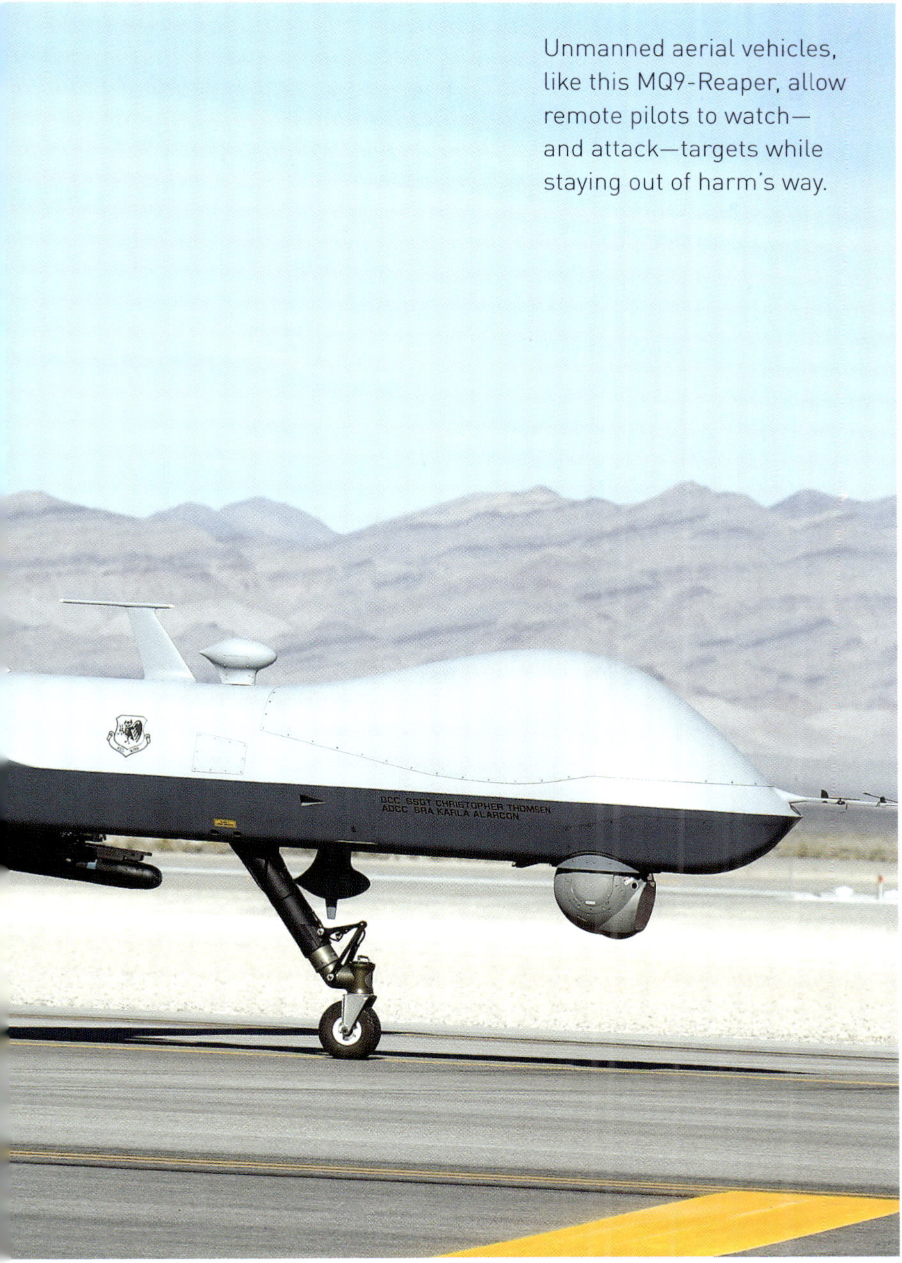

Unmanned aerial vehicles, like this MQ9-Reaper, allow remote pilots to watch—and attack—targets while staying out of harm's way.

light-footprint warfare sometimes occurs in the shadows. There is not always public awareness that a war is even taking place.

One of the most famous light-footprint operations was the killing of Osama bin Laden in 2011 in Pakistan—a country the United States was not at war with. A team of Navy SEALs was flown by helicopter into Pakistan undetected. They landed at a house where bin Laden was suspected of living and engaged in a battle with armed men there. In the end, bin Laden was killed. Even though one helicopter broke down, the Navy SEALs escaped Pakistan before the Pakistani military could respond.

While the daring raid to kill bin Laden captured headlines around the world, most light-footprint operations receive little attention. Bombs are dropped on people, and special forces raids kill high-value targets with some frequency around the world. Unless there are many civilian deaths or a soldier dies, these operations are not front-page news.

Cyberwarfare

A new kind of military force that poses a threat around the world is cyberwarfare. Cyberwarfare is when a country or group uses technology to attack another country or group. There are many cyberwarfare targets. One area at risk is a country's infrastructure. Infrastructure includes the network of water, electricity, and transportation that lets a country function. Since all of these systems are computerized, it is possible for an attack to bring them to a halt for a time.

While a large cyberattack has never affected a country's infrastructure, there have been several famous cyberattacks. The nuclear program of Iran, which the United States fears is being used to develop nuclear weapons, was hit by a computer virus called Stuxnet. Stuxnet caused heavy machinery to damage itself and set back the nuclear program a great deal. While no country has accepted responsibility, most analysts believe the United States was responsible—and perhaps other countries as well.

During the 2016 election cycle in the United States, Russia launched a coordinated cyberattack. It hacked the Democratic National Committee and leaked private documents. According to the FBI, the goal was to undermine confidence in the American democratic system. By trying to influence the election, Russian efforts challenged the foundation of democracy: that the outcome of an election represents the will of the people.

In this new era of cyberattacks, democracies around the world must decide how to respond. Should cyberattacks be met with military force? So far, no country has responded with bombs or soldiers when they are the victim of a cyberattack. Yet many world leaders have noted that physical attacks are a possibility if a cyberattack is serious enough.

Dilemmas Today

Cyberattacks, airstrikes, cross-border raids, and wars are currently taking place around the world. Questions about when military force is legal and how it should be used are important to think about and debate. There are no easy answers to these questions.

Issues surrounding military force are especially important for Americans to consider because the United States plays a key role in many conflicts. While the president and military direct military force, American citizens can also make their voices heard. It is the responsibility of citizens in democracies everywhere to discuss these issues and understand that the dilemmas of military force are pressing concerns that have the potential to cost thousands of people their lives.

CHAPTER 2

America's Use of Force

How and why the United States uses military force has changed throughout its history. When the country first gained independence from Great Britain, the United States was a small nation separated from the great powers of Europe by the Atlantic Ocean. Today, it is the world's only superpower, home of the most powerful military. As the United States grows and changes, its attitudes toward military force change as well. Events like the controversial Vietnam War have left their mark on society. America's history still shapes the modern debates about military force.

Evolving Attitudes

Early in its history, the United States used military force much less frequently than it does today. There was no large standing army of soldiers ready to fight around the world. The policy of the country was, in the words of Thomas Jefferson, "Peace, commerce, and honest friendship with all nations—

Opposite: The B-2 Spirit stealth bomber is nearly impossible to detect with radar. Advanced technologies give the United States an advantage on the battlefield.

entangling alliances with none." Washington, Jefferson, and other early presidents believed that the United States should avoid alliances with European powers. This would let the new country grow without drawing it into wars.

Nonetheless, the United States was not afraid to use military force early in its history. While Jefferson did not want to be entangled in foreign wars, he used military force when it was necessary. When pirates based in North Africa threatened American shipping, Jefferson sent troops to fight them. Similarly, the United States fought a series of wars against neighboring Native Americans to secure land. The United States was by no means pacifist—avoiding all military force—but its leaders did not think it should take part in conflicts not closely tied to its interests.

Some early American wars were still quite controversial. In 1846, the Mexican-American War broke out over a boundary dispute. Many Americans and one of the two major political parties of the era viewed the war as a war of aggression by American president James K. Polk. Political opposition to the war was fierce. Famous American intellectuals like Ralph Waldo Emerson also came out publicly against the conflict. Despite this, the war raged on until Mexico surrendered, and the United States gained a large amount of land, including California, from its victory.

At the beginning of both World War I and World War II in the 1900s, the United States tried to remain neutral. The American government and people did not want to get involved in distant wars. The use of military force and the lives and money they required were judged too costly. Nonetheless, the country eventually entered both World Wars when neutrality became impossible due to changing circumstances.

The Cold War

During World War II, the United States fought on the same side as the Soviet Union. The Soviet Union was a communist state centered in Russia. According to the ideals of communism, the

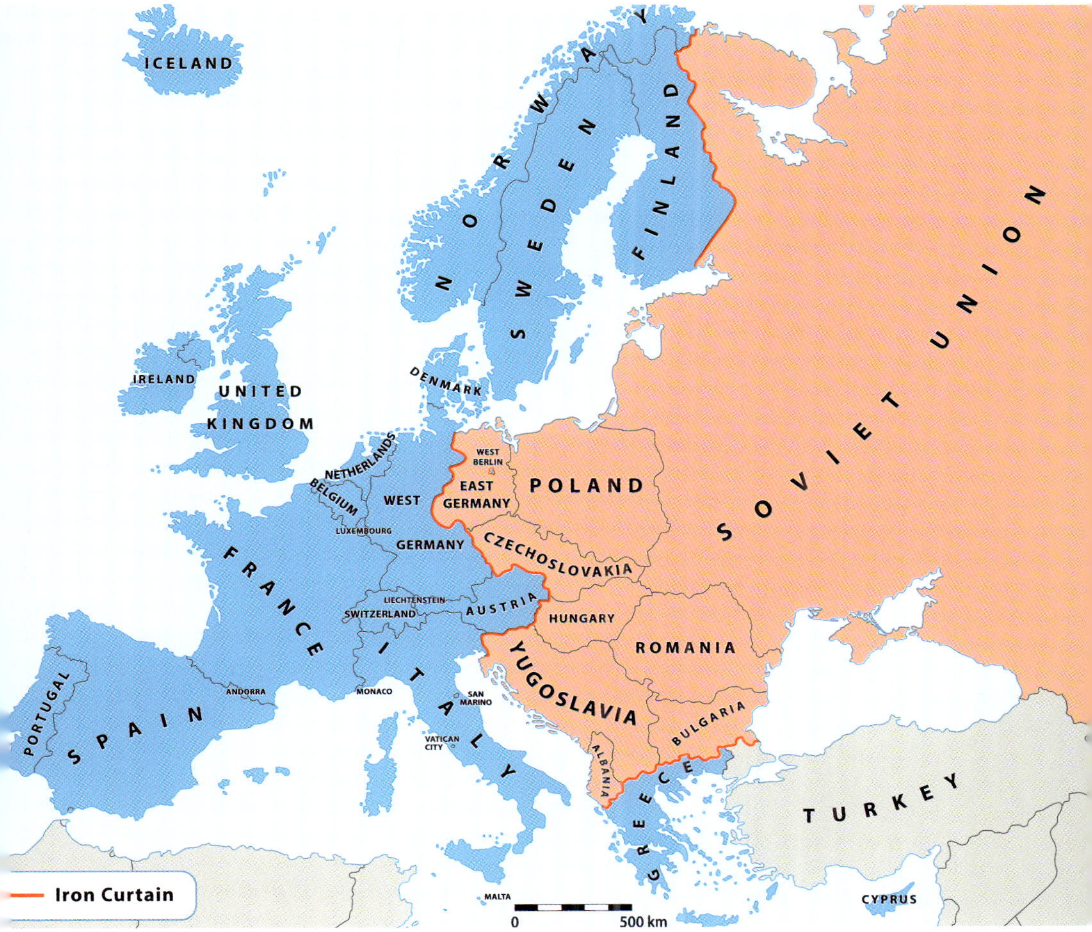

During the Cold War, the so-called Iron Curtain divided European countries that were allied with the Soviet Union (in red) from those that were allied with the United States (*in blue*).

rich should not control the means of production—factories and land for farming. Instead, the people should. The Soviet Union was also a totalitarian state, meaning the government held total power and controlled the lives of its citizens, whose rights were restricted.

The United States and Soviet Union were brought together by having a common enemy, Nazi Germany, during World War II. When the war ended, so did the alliance between the two superpowers. The world was largely split into two spheres. On the one side was the United States and its allies that later formed NATO. On the other stood the Soviet Union and the countries it controlled in Eastern Europe after forcing the Germans out during World War II. Politicians in America soon said there was a "free world" led by the United States, and a Communist Bloc without individual rights under Soviet control.

This led to a new level of American involvement in the affairs of the world. A heated debate occurred in the American government over how to respond to the Soviet Union. Both the United States and the Soviet Union had nuclear weapons, making open warfare between them impossible. The risk of a nuclear war that would end human civilization was too great.

The United States opted instead for a policy of "containment." The goal was that Communism would be contained in its borders and not allowed to expand. To achieve this goal, arms and money were sent by the United States to countries fighting communist rebels.

The policy of containment was put to the test in the countries of Korea and Vietnam. Both countries were divided with a communist government in the north and a pro-American government in the south. The communist governments eventually invaded their southern neighbors. This occurred first in Korea in 1950 and later in Vietnam.

The United States was forced to make a choice: watch pro-American governments fall to communism or send combat troops. It was a decision that many presidents wrestled with. The American public took part in these debates. The central question was if it was worth sending American soldiers to fight and die in a war aimed at stopping the spread of communism. (Ultimately, American soldiers were sent to both countries.) In Korea, the war was over in just over three years. A stalemate was achieved and Korea is still split between north and south.

In Vietnam, the war was much more difficult to end. Over the eight years that America was involved in combat operations there, the debate over military force took on new dimensions. Civilian casualties rose and became public through graphic photographs of the terrible human suffering of war. American men were drafted into the military in large numbers. Journalists began to say what many people suspected: the war showed no signs of being won, and North Vietnam was not going to stop fighting. As a result, public opposition to the war grew stronger and stronger. Most Americans no longer believed that using military force to stop the spread of Communism in Vietnam was worth the cost. The United States eventually withdrew, and South Vietnam fell soon after.

In 1991, the Cold War ended with the fall of the Soviet Union. Stopping the spread of Communism was no longer a justification for war. Nevertheless, the public backlash of the Vietnam War still shapes American debates about the use of military force.

EM5

In Vietnam, US Marines take part in an operation to clear an area of enemy combatants.

Modern Conflicts

Between the end of the Cold War and the beginning of the war on terror, the United States took part in several conflicts, such as the Gulf War. These conflicts were short lived and had few American casualties. Often, air power was the deciding factor, and there were limited engagements on the ground.

The 9/11 terror attacks marked a sharp increase in the use of American military force. The invasions of Afghanistan and Iraq involved hundreds of thousands of American combat troops. Fighting was fierce against an enemy that preferred to ambush American soldiers rather than commit to large battles. To date, more than 2,400 American soldiers have died in Afghanistan, and

American soldiers took part in fierce house-to-house fighting in the Iraqi city of Fallujah in 2004.

4,800 in Iraq. Many more have been wounded. Civilian deaths are impossible to count exactly, but well over 100,000 Afghan and Iraqi civilians lost their lives in the conflicts.

As part of the war on terror today, American soldiers are engaged in combat operations in seven countries: Afghanistan, Iraq, Syria, Yemen, Somalia, Libya, and Niger. The enemy in all of these places are Islamic extremists: people who believe in a warped version of Islam that celebrates violence. For the most part, American troops today are not expected to be on the front lines daily, as they were previously in Iraq and Afghanistan. Instead, they are meant to train local forces to fight terrorists, gather intelligence, and support airstrikes against the enemy by protecting bases. Occasional raids by special forces against high-value targets, like Osama bin Laden, also occur.

Debating the War on Terror

Although it began in 2001, the war on terror is still controversial. Most Americans supported the war in Afghanistan, yet public opinion eventually turned against the Iraq War. Elsewhere around the world, operations have been low profile. Occasionally, a story breaks about a conflict involving American troops, but often the public is unaware of where American soldiers are operating.

This was the case on October 4, 2017, when four American soldiers died in an ambush in the West African country of Niger. Most Americans did not know soldiers were even in the region until the story broke. Months later, the US government revealed there had been ten previous attacks against American forces in Niger that went unreported. The public is often kept in the dark about small-scale deployments in the war on terror. When there are American casualties overseas, it often reignites long-standing

Torture

During the war on terror, controversial techniques have been used to interrogate suspected terrorists. Critics say these tactics qualify as torture. American president Barack Obama has also said that, in his opinion, some of the techniques were torture. However, some American officials continue to deny that their methods can be classified that way.

The most well-known and controversial interrogation technique is called waterboarding. Waterboarding involves holding cloth over a person's face and pouring water over it, causing the victim to feel like they are drowning. People who are waterboarded experience extreme feelings of terror and pain. Waterboarding took place during the presidency of George W. Bush, but Barack Obama ended the practice. There is a widespread consensus that the practice constitutes torture.

Nonetheless, the debate over whether to torture suspected terrorists continues to the present. President Trump said he would bring back waterboarding when campaigning for office, but he has not done so as of 2018. The debate over torture centers on two key questions: Is torture an effective way to get information and, if so, should it be used despite the fact it is against international laws that the United States has signed?

A Senate report on the use of torture found that it was not an effective way to get information. This is also the position of many law enforcement agencies around the world. One issue torture presents is that victims will tell lies if they believe the torture will stop. When the goal is accurate information, this is problematic. Many citizens and many politicians say torture should be banned

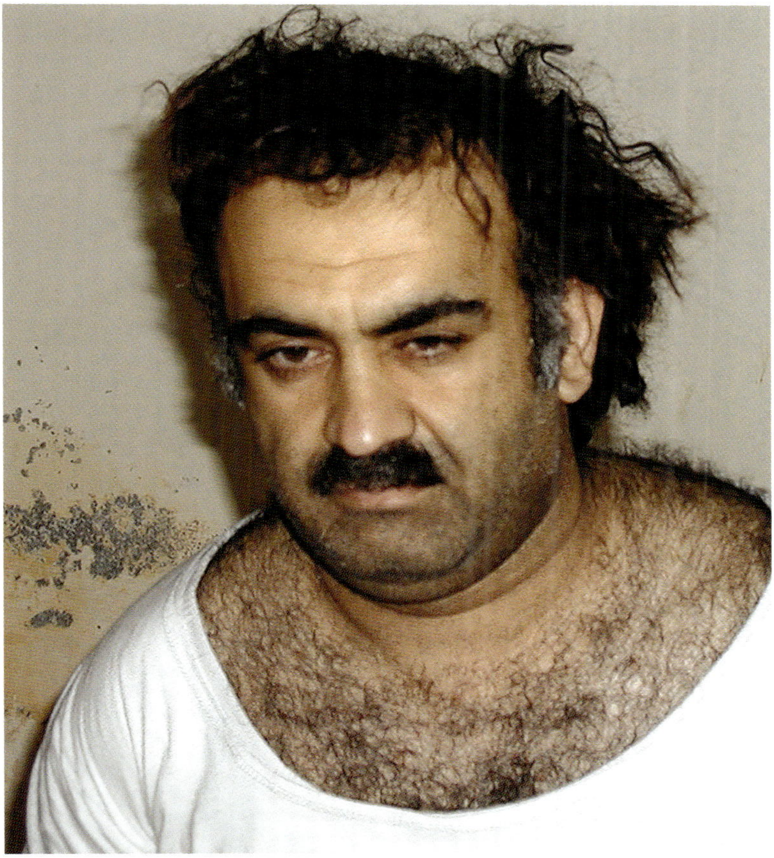

Khalid Sheikh Mohammed, who planned the 9/11 terror attacks, was waterboarded more than any other detainee. A Senate report documented fifteen waterboarding sessions.

regardless of its effectiveness. It is against the UN Conventions Against Torture that the United States agreed to. They also worry it fuels anti-American feelings around the world when graphic details of torture emerge.

The deployment of American soldiers to the country of Niger was largely unknown until the 2017 ambush.

debates. The main question asked is if the war on terror actually makes Americans safer.

According to supporters of the conflict, the war on terror prevents terror attacks by killing high-level targets, making terror networks less effective. They point to successful strikes against al-Qaeda, the network Osama bin Laden headed. Drone strikes, arrests, and military operations have neutralized important al-Qaeda leaders around the world. The terror group has never again launched an attack nearly as large as 9/11.

Opponents of the war on terror argue that it makes Americans less safe. The use of airstrikes—and the civilian casualties they cause—as well as the past use of torture has eroded American standing in the world, they say. Many people no longer see the nation as a beacon of liberty and justice. Along with the long-term military occupation of Iraq, these actions have inspired many combatants to take up arms against the United States. People who see images of dead civilians in their country and read of torture are more likely to think they are doing the right thing by fighting. Additionally, American troops are in their countries and easy to reach.

Critics of the war on terror argue that if you look at the numbers, it is obvious the war has increased, not decreased, terrorism. According to Robert A. Pape writing for *Foreign Policy*: "From 1980 to 2003, there were 343 suicide attacks around the world, and at most 10 percent were anti-American inspired. Since 2004 [to October of 2010], there have been more than 2,000, over 91 percent against US and allied forces in Afghanistan, Iraq, and other countries."

Iraqis carry the coffins of civilians who lost their lives during an American operation in Baghdad.

Not Declaring War

Another controversial aspect of the war on terror is its legal basis in the United States. According to the Constitution, it is Congress, not the president, that declares war. In recent history, many wars have been fought without an official declaration of war. To prevent the president from fighting wars without congressional approval, the War Powers Resolution was passed in 1973. This law states that the president must notify Congress within forty-eight hours of using force to protect the United States, and American forces must be withdrawn in sixty days unless Congress has approved their deployment.

Today, the War Powers Resolution has not been able to prevent presidents from using military force against the wishes of Congress. This is largely due to a law passed after the 9/11 terror attacks called the 2001 Authorization for Use of Military Force (AUMF). This law gave the president permission to use military force to strike against those responsible for 9/11. Presidents George W. Bush and Barack Obama justified the use of military force in fourteen different countries based on the AUMF, according to a 2016 government report.

In other words, the president is free to use military force without getting congressional approval today if it is arguable that force is in response to 9/11. Critics, including some American congresspeople, say this is unconstitutional. There have been some efforts to repeal—or get rid of—the 2001 AUMF in Congress, but so far they have been unsuccessful.

Many citizens and politicians worry that the president's power has become too broad. The deployment of American soldiers in countries around the world as part of the war on terror is subject to little congressional oversight. For instance, when the four American soldiers died in the 2017 ambush in Niger, some US senators even expressed surprise that soldiers were in the country. The use of American military force is so pervasive that members of Congress do not know all the countries American soldiers are fighting in.

Barack Obama, George W. Bush, and their wives mark the tenth anniversary of 9/11. The terror attacks defined the foreign policy of both presidents.

Difficult Decisions

Since 2015, the US military has been active in seventy-six countries during the war on terror, according to a report by Brown University's Watson Institute for International and Public Affairs. That is nearly 40 percent of countries in the world. This military activity around the world shows no signs of slowing down.

As American deployments of military force continue, so too will debates over America's rights and responsibilities. Questions about whether force makes Americans safer and whether it is worth the cost in lives and money are difficult to answer. The United States is not unique is facing these dilemmas. Other democracies around the world do as well.

The Constitution and the Military

Who controls the military is outlined in the US Constitution, with responsibility split between the president and Congress. According to the Constitution, "The President shall be the Commander in Chief of the Army and Navy of the United States." The president oversees military action and issues orders to military commanders. Meanwhile, Congress has the power "To declare War ... and make Rules concerning Captures on Land and Water; To raise and support Armies ... To provide and maintain a Navy." Congress decides when to declare war and controls the money spent to support the military.

The fact that Congress and the president share oversight of the military is important. Ideally, neither one can use military force without the other's approval. Furthermore, this structure is an example of civilian control of the military. Politicians are civilians, not soldiers, and they are elected to office.

Civilian control of the military means that the military generals and soldiers are told what to do by politicians. Generals are not free to start or wage wars. Civilian control of the military is a cornerstone of modern democracy. Unlike soldiers, politicians are voted into office by the people. Voters can hold them accountable by not voting for them again.

CHAPTER 3

Military Force Around the World

Although it was started by the United States, the war on terror has drawn in other countries from around the world. American allies have been faced with the difficult decision of how to navigate the conflict. Most were willing to help in Afghanistan. A few sent soldiers to Iraq. Yet allies in democratic nations struggle to balance their alliance with the United States with the unpopularity of many aspects of the war on terror, such as the invasion of Iraq and the torture of captured terrorists.

Dilemmas in Canada

Canada's involvement in the war on terror spotlights the difficult decisions that countries around the world face during a conflict. After the 9/11 terror attacks, Canada immediately pledged to help its ally the United States. As a member of

Opposite: British soldiers, like this Royal Marine, fought in Iraq beside American troops.

Canadian soldiers survey their surroundings at a forward operating base in Kandahar, Afghanistan, in 2006.

NATO, it was obligated to come to the defense of the United States when NATO invoked its promise of mutual self-defense.

Canadian soldiers were some of the first to set foot in Afghanistan, and the public supported the war there. However, when the United States decided to invade Iraq, the situation was far less clear. Less than a third of Canadians supported a US-led invasion without authorization from the UN. When the UN refused to back the invasion, Canada informed the United States it would not send troops.

The decision to send combat troops to Afghanistan but not Iraq was widely debated in Canada. It raised questions of how far the country should go to help an ally. Canadians worried that angering the United States was risky. The United States is Canada's largest trading partner and only neighboring country by land. In the end, the US government did not respond harshly to Canada's refusal to help in Iraq. In part, this was due to Canada's strong commitment to the war in Afghanistan. That commitment lasted for many years, but it eventually came to an end.

By September 2008, a CBC News poll found that just 41 percent of Canadians approved of the country's participation in the war in Afghanistan. That same month, Prime Minister Steven Harper announced that Canadian combat operations there would end in 2011. After keeping the scheduled withdrawal date, some Canadian troops stayed in noncombat roles until 2014. For twelve years, Canada was involved in the war. At its end, 158 Canadian soldiers and seven Canadian civilians had lost their lives.

The Military as a Threat to Democracy

Nearly all democracies have some sort of military. Armed forces help safeguard a democracy's independence from other countries. Civilian control of the armed forces is supposed to guarantee that the military is controlled by the government—and not the other way around. Nevertheless, the military has sometimes proved fatal to democratic governments. The overthrow of a government is called a coup d'état, or simply "coup."

Throughout history, many democratic governments have ended due to coups. Often, it is the military, or a small group of officers, that seizes power. In this way, the military force that a democratic country's people are supposed to control is used against them.

There has never been in a coup in the United States or Canada, but military takeovers plague some democracies. Pakistan is one Asian country with a history of coups disrupting its democratic government. In 1947, Pakistan gained independence from Great Britain as a democratic state. However, in 1958, Ayub Khan, leader of the Pakistani Army, seized power. Since then, power has repeatedly switched between democratically-elected civilian leaders and military officers that take it by force.

Pakistani president Ayub Khan, pictured here in 1960, launched the first coup in his country's history. Other Pakistani military leaders would later follow his example.

The bodies of three Canadian soldiers killed in Afghanistan return home on December 8, 2008.

Funding the Military

Countries that want to keep open the option of military force must spend money. Otherwise, if they decide to use military force, their soldiers may be undertrained, poorly equipped, or too few to complete the mission. For this reason, questions about how much money to give the military are central to debates about military force.

Some countries choose to have very small militaries. This makes it difficult for them to intervene in conflicts abroad. The ability to send and support soldiers across the world is not cheap. Partly for this reason, some countries decide military force is not worth investing in. For instance, the European country of Iceland has no army, but it is part of NATO. NATO guarantees its defense, and in return, Iceland plays nonmilitary roles in operations.

The United States spends a great deal of money on its military. In fact, the United States alone accounts for about one-third of the world's military spending. In 2017, America spent $610 billion, according to a report by the Stockholm International Peace Research Institute. The next two biggest spenders were China at $228 billion and Saudi Arabia at $69.4 billion.

The large amount of money that the United States spends makes the war on terror possible. Without this money, American soldiers, drones, ships, and aircraft could not operate around the globe. However, spending this much on the military is controversial. The federal government in Washington, DC, spends more money on the military than on services like education and transportation each year. Critics say some of the money that goes to the military should instead be used to benefit Americans at home.

Bashar al-Assad

In 2011, a wave of democratic protests swept across the Arab world. These protests became known as the Arab Spring. In the Middle Eastern country of Syria, dictator Bashar al-Assad responded to calls for greater freedom with military force. Demonstrators were killed. Many Syrians soon took up arms against Assad. Assad had been president since 2000 after winning a number of elections, but he was elected in name only. His father had ruled the country from 1971 to 2000, and no opposition to the ruling family was allowed.

Bashar al-Assad ruthlessly used the Syrian military against his own citizens. Bombs were dropped on cities that rebelled. Deadly chemical weapons—banned by the Geneva Conventions—were also used to kill civilians. Many different opposition groups soon fought Assad. Some were pro-democracy, but others were extremists. One extremist group, the Islamic State in Iraq and Syria (ISIS) soon captured a large area of land in Syria and neighboring Iraq. ISIS is also responsible for terror attacks around the globe.

Between 2014 and 2018, the United States launched airstrikes against ISIS in Syria. Despite calling for the removal of Assad from power, American forces were careful not to strike Assad's forces because he was supported by Russia, and Russian soldiers were also active in Syria. A confrontation between the United States and Russia—two countries with nuclear weapons—was to be avoided. On April 14, 2018, the United States did launch one strike on Assad's forces after chemical weapons were used on Syrian civilians.

Assad's brutal crackdown on his own people shows the negative impact military force can have. It also shows how difficult it can be for the world to respond to a humanitarian crisis. Russian support for Assad and the rise of terrorist groups in the country prevented the United States from doing much to defend Syrian civilians from Assad.

Syrian president Bashar al-Assad used his country's military forces to cling to power during the Syrian Civil War.

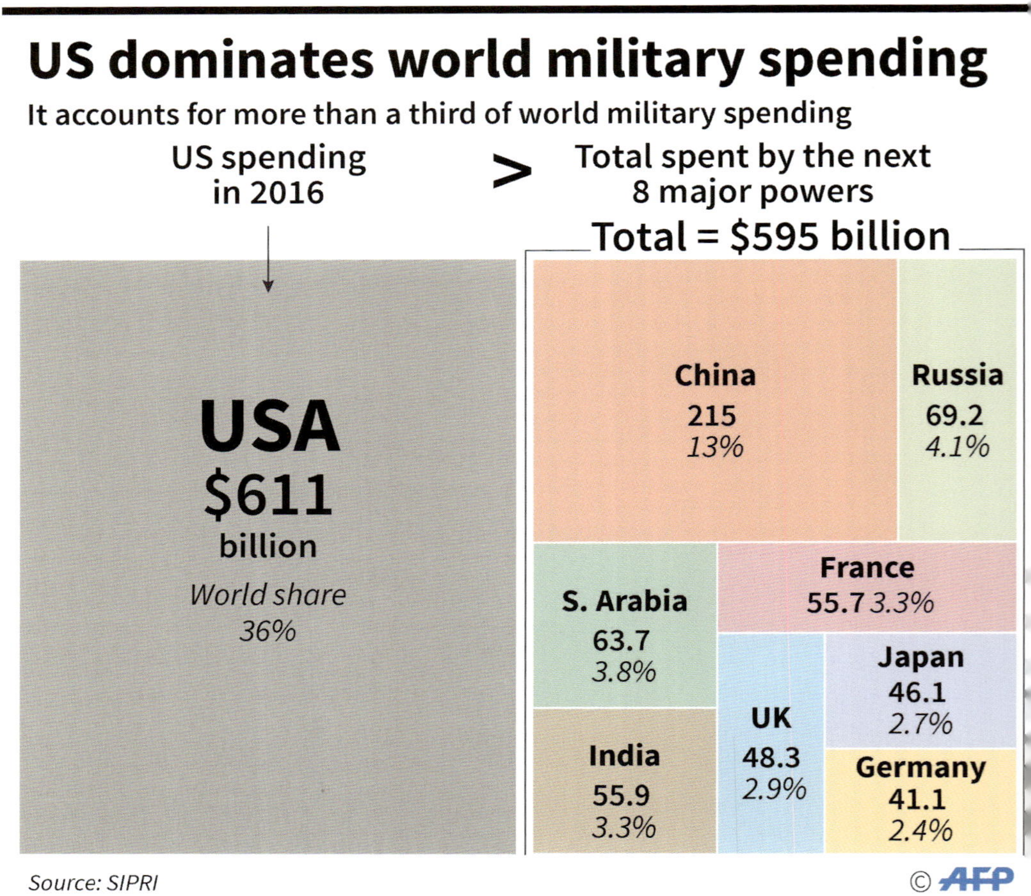

The United States spends more money on its military than the top eight other countries combined.

When the federal government makes its yearly budget, military spending is often debated. Some lawmakers want cuts to military spending so that money can be spent elsewhere. Others warn that the military is underfunded. Due to the war on terror, there are concerns that the United States is not prepared for a major war with another country. Much of the military is now geared toward countering terrorism and not other state-of-the-art militaries.

Debates over military spending often reflect attitudes toward military force in general. People who do not believe the war on terror makes Americans safer are quick to criticize its huge cost in money and lives. Going forward, there are sure to be debates in Washington, DC, and other capitals around the world over how much to spend on the military. Citizens fund the military and government through their tax dollars, so their voice is an important one in these debates over how much to spend.

Each new Gerald R. Ford–class aircraft carrier costs about thirteen billion dollars. Aircraft carriers allow the United States to fly aircraft in regions where they cannot access airports.

I WON'T FIGHT IN VIETNAM
OR ANY WHERE ELSE
End the War In Vietna Now

CHAPTER 4

The Power of the People

The president and Congress direct military force, but that does not mean people cannot participate in debates about military force. The United States has a long history of individuals and groups trying to change America's military policies. The most straightforward way to seek change is to support and vote for politicians who agree with your views. However, street protests and other means are also used.

Anti-War Movements in America

Even before the United States was a country, there were anti-war movements in the American colonies. At that time, anti-war feelings were usually due to religious beliefs. Quakers—members of a small Christian group—are pacifists. Pacifists believe military force is never justified. During the Revolutionary War, Quakers refused not only to fight on either side but also to pay taxes since tax money was used to fight the war. This tradition of tax resistance to oppose war has

Opposite: Protesters march against the Vietnam War in 1965.

been used throughout American history to the present day. A small number of people refuse to pay their taxes and even go to prison for it rather than help fund the military.

When the Mexican-American War broke out in 1846, a new kind of anti-war movement materialized. Many American intellectuals and politicians opposed the war not because they were pacifists but because they thought it was unjust. They believed the president had engineered the war to take lands from Mexico. The most famous protester was Henry David Thoreau, a writer from Massachusetts. He spent a night in jail rather than pay a tax.

Up until the 1960s, anti-war protests tended to be individual or held by small groups of pacifists. Protesters had never succeeded in altering the course of a conflict. That changed with American involvement in the Vietnam War. As the United States became more and more involved in the Cold War conflict, many Americans turned against the war. Anti-war protests drew tens of thousands of people and took place across the country. They sometimes turned violent. This was the case at Kent State University in 1970 when National Guardsmen fired into a crowd of protesting students, killing two protesters and two students walking to class nearby. That year, colleges across the country shut down to prevent further violence. The peace movement was a major disruption to the country and helped ensure an American withdrawal from Vietnam.

As George W. Bush considered invading Iraq in 2002, anti-war protests broke out across the United States and in cities around the world. People took to the streets carrying signs and making their opinions known. Protests were a clear message to lawmakers and the president that many people did not support the proposed invasion. Although the protests did not stop the invasion of Iraq, they did give people a voice. After the invasion, protests continued until the withdrawal of American forces.

Boycott

Protests are usually aimed at changing the policy of the country they take place in. Protests mostly work through disrupting the day-to-day running of a country or by signaling that voters are unhappy. Sometimes, protests may express displeasure at a foreign country's choices, but these bring little pressure to bear on a country when they take place outside its borders.

To pressure foreign governments, peace activists have turned to other techniques: boycott and divestment. Boycott and divestment are a refusal to do business with a country and companies in it. This applied economic pressure aims to force the foreign government into changing its mind on some issue.

The first major international boycott was against South Africa in the 1970s and 1980s. At that time, apartheid—a system of racial segregation—existed in South Africa. Whites were given more rights than blacks, who were abused by the state. The boycott campaign against South Africa helped lead to the collapse of apartheid when the United States government backed it. South Africa's economy suffered until the nation abolished apartheid.

Today, Israel is the main target of boycott attempts. Its long-running conflict with the Palestinian territories is controversial. The BDS movement (Boycott, Divestment, and Sanctions) encourages celebrities and academics not to visit Israel. It also encourages ordinary people and businesses not to buy goods from companies that operate in Israeli settlements. These Israeli settlements—built on land the UN recognizes as part of the Palestinian territories—are the major target of the BDS movement. Opponents of the settlements say they make peace between Israel and the Palestinian territories impossible. Supporters say the UN ought to recognize them as part of Israel.

Guantanamo Bay

When the war on terror began, president George W. Bush was faced with a decision about what to do with captured enemies. Many were imprisoned in the countries they were captured in, primarily Afghanistan and Iraq. However, foreigners suspected of being terrorists were often taken into US custody and moved to an American prison in Cuba, Guantanamo Bay. In all, at least 779 people have been detained there, including 21 children. Many former detainees and American personnel say inmates were abused at the facility.

Detainees are often held at Guantanamo without trial or access to a lawyer. The government argues these constitutional rights do not extend to Guantanamo prisoners because they are not American. At the same time, they say detainees are not due protection under the Geneva Convention, the laws that protect prisoners of war. Instead, detainees are labeled "unlawful enemy combatants," and due no protection under American or international law. President Obama reversed some of these decisions, but little changed in the lives of many detainees. Some are still held there with slim chances of release.

Guantanamo became a lightning rod for criticism about American abuses during the war on terror. People around the country and the world protested the detention of people without ever charging them under the law or telling them what crime they were accused of. Protesters often wore orange jumpsuits and black hoods over their heads, mimicking what detainees are forced to wear.

Protesters wear prison jumpsuits and carry the names of people held at Guantanamo Bay on May 27, 2008.

BOYCOTT
SOUTH AFRICAN
GOODS - LOOK FOR THE LABEL

On March 19, 1963, Londoners rallied against the government of South Africa and its racist laws by encouraging a boycott of the country's goods.

The BDS movement is quite controversial in the United States. Pro-Israel groups and lawmakers have tried to prevent companies from joining it through legislation. An Anti-Boycott Act has been introduced in Congress, but so far has not been passed. Supporters say it would protect Israel, a close American ally, from the BDS movement. Critics say that making boycott illegal restricts freedom of speech. If it passes, companies that have publicly said they supported the boycott could be fined by the US government.

While the modern BDS movement is controversial, boycott as a tactic to pressure foreign governments is less so. It is one of the few ways a foreign citizen can make their opinion clear, and it remains a technique that peace activists can use to oppose foreign military force.

What You Can Do

In addition to engaging in protests and boycotts, you can make your voice heard through the democratic process: helping politicians you support get elected, writing letters to your representatives in Congress, and voting once you turn eighteen years old. These are all ways that you can help shape the country.

Before you try to change things, you need to decide your own opinions about when and how your country should use military force. Debates about what keeps us safe and which conflicts are worth their cost in lives and money are difficult to answer. Having an opinion on these important matters is part of your responsibility as a citizen of a democracy. Lawmakers are supposed to represent the people. If you do not make your voice heard, they will not know what you believe.

Staying Informed

Many conflicts are ongoing throughout the world. The American-led war on terror is just one example and involves dozens of countries. Soldiers, drones, and planes from various nations participate to different degrees, depending on the country. This involvement often changes quickly.

The rapidly evolving nature of modern war makes staying informed critically important. The media does not always cover deployments of American military force in a country unless there are high-profile casualties among soldiers or civilians. The frontpage of websites and newspapers may not even run stories about the war on terror since it has been going on for so long.

These circumstances make it essential to read many different news sources. Looking at just one source is not enough. It is helpful to also look at well-respected international sources, such as the BBC. International publications can provide a more neutral look at American news. Reading widely can expose you to different ideas and ensure that you see current events. Even if one media outlet does not cover a troop deployment to a new country, others might.

A California woman votes in the 2016 election. Voting is one way Americans can influence their government.

VOTE

GLOSSARY

aggressor The country that begins a conflict by attacking first.

airstrike An attack carried out by military aircraft using bombs, missiles, or guns.

allies Countries with an agreement to protect each other's interests.

casualty A person who is killed or wounded.

civilian A person who is not in the military.

convoy A caravan of vehicles protected by troops.

cyberattack An attack on a computer network or system. Cyberattacks can be carried out by countries, individuals, or groups.

dictator A person who wields total control over a country.

humanitarian In the interest of people's wellbeing.

interrogate To question a person.

national interest The survival and protection of a country and its economic goals.

Navy SEALS A special operations force of the US Navy. Navy SEALS are highly trained soldiers who complete difficult missions.

oversight The action of supervising an activity.

pacifist Someone who believes that war and violence are always wrong.

regime change To replace a government with a new one.

repeal To reverse a law.

rules of engagement Rules a country makes for its military.

sanction To apply penalties to a country or its leaders.

unmanned aerial vehicle (UAV) Commonly known as drones, UAVs in the military are capable of firing missiles at and bombing targets on the ground.

veto The ability to block a decision.

FURTHER INFORMATION

Books

Coster, Patience. *The Ethics of War*. Both Sides of the Story. New York: Rosen Publishing, 2012.

Miller, Mara. *The Iraq War: A Controversial War in Perspective*. Issues in Focus Today. Berkeley Heights, NJ: Enslow, 2010.

New York Times Editorial Staff. *War*. Changing Perspectives. New York: Rosen Publishing, 2019.

Websites

NATO on the Map

https://www.nato.int/nato-on-the-map

An interactive map shows current NATO operations and member countries.

PBS News Hour: Afghanistan War

https://www.pbs.org/newshour/tag/afghanistan-war

PBS News Hour presents a round-up of recent articles about the conflict in Afghanistan.

Videos

President George W. Bush Addresses a Joint Congress About the War on Terror

https://www.youtube.com/watch?v=9vzRMaHCysU

Watch the speech President George W. Bush delivered to both houses of Congress on September 20, 2001.

Sound Smart: Vietnam War Protests

https://www.youtube.com/watch?v=G3slnPIh_oU

Historian Yohuru Williams explains the importance of protests during the Vietnam War.

What Was the War Powers Resolution of 1973?

https://www.youtube.com/watch?v=barQHoh3krc

History.com looks at the history of the War Powers Resolution and why the law was passed.

BIBLIOGRAPHY

BBC News. "Syrian President Bashar al-Assad: Facing Down Rebellion." September 3, 2018. https://www.bbc.com/news/10338256.

Brown, Adrian. "Osama bin Laden's Death: How It Happened." BBC News, September 10, 2012. https://www.bbc.com/news/world-south-asia-13257330.

CBC News. "Public Support for Afghan Mission Lowest Ever; Poll." September 5, 2008. https://www.cbc.ca/news/canada/public-support-for-afghan-mission-lowest-ever-poll-1.707644.

Goldsmith, Jack, and Matthew Waxman. "The Legal Legacy of Light-Footprint Warfare." *Washington Quarterly* 39, no. 2 (2016): 7–21.

Hains, Tim. "ACLU Warns: Post 9/11 AUMF Gives President Trump 'Blank Check' for Unlimited Worldwide War." *Real Clear Politics*, April 18, 2018. https://www.realclearpolitics.com/video/2018/04/18/aclu_warns_post-911_aumf_gives_president_trump_blank_check_for_unlimited_worldwide_war.html.

Hakimi, Monica. "The Jus Ad Bellum's Regulatory Form." *American Journal of International Law* 112, no. 2 (2018): 151–190.

Miller, Leila. "Facing a Russian Cyber Attack, Obama Officials Struggled to Respond." *PBS*, October 31, 2017. https://www.pbs.org/wgbh/frontline/article/facing-a-russian-cyber-attack-obama-officials-struggled-to-respond.

NPR. "Is It Time to End the War on Terror?" September 13, 2011. https://www.npr.org/2011/09/13/140342312/is-it-time-to-end-the-war-on-terror.

Pape, Robert A. "It's the Occupation, Stupid." *Foreign Policy*, October 18, 2010. https://foreignpolicy.com/2010/10/18/its-the-occupation-stupid.

Savage, Charlie, Eric Schmitt, and Thomas Gibbons-Neff. "U.S. Kept Silent About Its Role in Another Firefight in Niger." *New York Times*, March 14, 2018. https://www.nytimes.com/2018/03/14/world/africa/niger-green-berets-isis-firefight-december.html.

Tian, Nan, Aude Fleurant, Alexandra Kuimova, Pieter D. Wezeman, and Siemon T. Wezeman. "Trends in World Military Expenditure, 2017." *SIPRI Fact Sheet*. Solna, Sweden: Stockholm International Peace Research Institute, 2017.

Ward, Alex. "The Senate Is Moving Closer to Ending US Support for the War in Yemen." *Vox*, November 28, 2018. https://www.vox.com/2018/11/28/18116442/yemen-war-powers-senate-vote-sanders.

Zenko, Micah. "The Big Lie About the Libyan War." *Foreign Policy*, March 22, 2016. https://foreignpolicy.com/2016/03/22/libya-and-the-myth-of-humanitarian-intervention.

INDEX

Page numbers in **boldface** refer to images.

ABOUT THE AUTHOR

Derek Miller is a writer and educator from Salisbury, Maryland. He is the author of more than a dozen books for middle school and high school students, including *Dilemmas in Democracy: Military Force* and *Dilemmas in Democracy: Voter Disenfranchisement*. In his free time, Miller enjoys reading and traveling with his wife.